Publisher's note:

Tintin, the intrepid reporter, first made his appearance January 10, 1929, in a serial newspaper strip with an adventure in the Soviet Union. From there, it was on to the Belgian Congo and then to America. Together with his dog, Snowy; an old seaman, Captain Haddock; an eccentric professor, Cuthbert Calculus; look-alike detectives, Thomson and Thompson; and others, Tintin roamed the world from one adventure to the next.

Tintin's dog, Snowy, a small white fox terrier, converses with Tintin, saves his life many times, and acts as his confidant, despite his weakness for whiskey and a tendency toward greediness. Captain Haddock, in some ways Snowy's counterpart, is a reformed lover of whiskey, with a tendency toward colorful language and a desire to be a gentleman-farmer. Cuthbert Calculus, a hard-of-hearing, sentimental, absent-minded professor, goes from small-time inventor to nuclear physicist. The detectives, Thomson and Thompson, stereotyped characters down to their old-fashioned bowler hats and outdated expressions, are always chasing Tintin. Their attempts at dressing in the costume of the place they are in make them stand out all the more.

The Adventures of Tintin appeared in newspapers and books all over the world. Georges Remi (1907–1983), better known as Hergé, based Tintin's adventures on his own interest in and knowledge of places around the world. The stories were often irreverent, frequently political and satirical, and always exciting and humorous.

Tintin's Travel Diaries is a new series, inspired by Hergé's characters and based on notebooks Tintin may have kept as he traveled. Each book in this series takes the reader to a different country, exploring its geography, and the customs, the culture, and the heritage of the people living there. Hergé's original cartooning is used, juxtaposed with photographs showing the country as it is today, to give a feeling of fun as well as education.

If Hergé's cartoons seem somewhat out of place in today's society, think of the time in which they were drawn. The cartoons reflect the thinking of the day, and set next to modern photographs, we learn something about ourselves and society, as well as about the countries Tintin explores. We can see how attitudes have changed over the course of half a century.

Hergé, himself, would change his stories and drawings periodically to reflect the changes in society and the comments his work would receive. For example, when it was originally written in 1930, Tintin in the Congo, on which Tintin's Travel Diaries: Africa is based, was slanted toward Belgium as the fatherland. When Hergé prepared a color version in 1946, he did away with this slant. Were Hergé alive today, he would probably change many other stereotypes that appear in his work.

From the Congo, Tintin went on to America. This was in 1931. Al Capone was notorious, and the idea of cowboys and Indians, prohibition, the wild west, as well as factories, all held a place of fascination.

Cigars of the Pharaoh (1934) introduced Hergé's fans to the mysteries of India. A trip to China came with The Blue Lotus in 1936, the first story Hergé thoroughly researched. After that, everything was researched, including revisions of previous stories.

Tintin's Travel Diaries are fun to read, fun to look at, and provide educational, enjoyable trips around the world. Perhaps, like Tintin, you, too, will be inspired to seek out new adventures!

The publisher particularly wishes to thank Mrs. Christine Ockrent and television channel Antenne 2 for their kind permission to use the title Travel Diaries.

THE UNITED STATES

TINTIN'S TRAVEL DIARIES

A collection conceived and produced by Martine Noblet.

Les films du sable thank the following **Connaissance du monde** photographers for their participation in this work:

Jean-Claude Berrier, Alain De La Porte, Michel Aubert, Christian Monty.

The authors thank Christiane Erard, Cathy Berrier, and Daniel De Bruyker for their collaboration.

First edition for the United States and Canada published by Barron's Educational Series, Inc., 1994

All inquiries should be addressed to:
Barron's Educational Series, Inc.
250 Wireless Boulevard
Hauppauge, New York 11788

Library of Congress Catalog Card No.: 94-10996
International Standard Book No. 0-8120-6428-3 (hardcover)
International Standard Book No. 0-8120-1867-2 (paperback)
Library of Congress Cataloging-in-Publication Data

Deltenre, Chantal.
    The United States / text by Chantal Deltenre and Martine Noblet; translation by Maureen Walker.
        p.   cm. — (Tintin's travel diaries)
    Includes bibliographical references and index.
    ISBN 0-8120-6428-3. —ISBN 0-8120-1867-2 (pbk.)
        1. United States—Description and travel—Juvenile literature. 2.Tintin (Fictitious character)—Juvenile literature. [1. United States. 2. Cartoons and comics.] I. Noblet, Martine. II. Title.   III. Series.
E169.04.D4413   1994
917.304'9—dc20   94-10996
                                                                          CIP
                                                                          AC

Printed in Hong Kong
56789   9927   98765432

THE UNITED STATES

Text by Chantal Deltenre and Martine Noblet
Translation by Maureen Walker

BARRON'S

Tintin: an old friendship, a long story. I met him around 1942, during the war [WWII]. He had already set off, in pictures, for America, but I hadn't. I was 17 years old and used to look after hundreds of kids in Paris who needed something to do on Sundays. I showed them Tintin's earliest adventures in black and white still photos that could be projected on a screen. We spent ten minutes looking at each drawing and telling the story. The kids would shout with joy and sing together, "Who's not afraid of anything, anything? It's Tintin! And who's the one who'll always follow, follow? It's Snowy!"

When the war was over, I followed him to America. A canoe trip from Quebec to New Orleans by way of the rivers and lakes, and the Mississippi River, with rapids to shoot, portages and swarms of mosquitoes—so many miles of paddling. There were four of us, good friends, and one day we outraced the Lake Huron Algonquins! In 1949 Hergé told our story in cartoons, in his *Tintin* paper. It was called "Canoeing Across America," and at the end Tintin himself congratulated us. Since then, I've continued to travel. Thanks, Tintin…

JEAN RASPAIL

When I was a fifteen-year-old, in short pants just like Tintin and all the other French boys in the 1940s, I used to daydream about visiting far-away America, with its skyscrapers and wide open prairies. But the world was at war and New York and San Francisco were cities that were still out of reach and hardly real to us.

When peace returned, I left for New York aboard a big transatlantic steamship and during that week on the ocean I experienced a wonderfully strange feeling of being out of one's element that travelers who today fly from one continent to another in seven hours can never know.

Like you, Tintin, I daydreamed on the shores of Lake Michigan. But, whereas you bravely confronted gangsters in Chicago, I escaped to the Far West to raft down the great Colorado River, ride a horse in the Rocky Mountains, and live for a time with the Navajo Indians. What a fantastic country!

Our paths often crossed on the trails of the New World that we both loved equally passionately, and for which I yearn as much as you do.

J. C. BERRIER

CONTENTS

Words in **boldface** in the text refer to the Glossary on page 70.

IS IT CALLED "AMERICA" OR "THE UNITED STATES"?

What some people call "America" is actually the United States of America. Located on the continent of North America between Canada and Mexico, it is so large that there are time differences from one area of the country to another.

The vast American continent is made up of two great continental masses: North America and South America, connected to each other by the Central American isthmus.

North America consists of three large countries: Canada, the United States, and Mexico. The territory of the United States, the fourth largest country in the world, is so large that when it is noon in New York on the east coast, it is only nine o'clock in the morning in Los Angeles on the west coast, and seven o'clock in the morning in Alaska or the Hawaiian Islands. So, if you're planning to make a phone call to someone in another part of the country, you'd better figure out what time it is there!

Because it is so vast, nearly all the world's climates and natural landscapes can be found somewhere in the United States. For instance, Florida and Louisiana in the South contain **alligator**-infested swamps that are similar to equatorial landscapes. In the Southwest, Texas is a hot, dry area, while in California, in the West, we find valleys with a mild climate next to hot, arid deserts. Farther north, New York, Boston, and other large cities often experience heat waves in summer and severe snowstorms in winter. Other areas, especially the mountainous regions of Wyoming and Colorado have very harsh climates. Alaska, located between Canada and Siberia, is polar country, and Hawaii is part of a tropical **archipelago** in the middle of the Pacific Ocean.

Top: Caribou in Alaska
Bottom Left: White Sands National Monument, New Mexico
Bottom Right: A camper in Baja California

WHAT ARE THE VARIOUS REGIONS OF THE UNITED STATES?

Although there are often cultural differences between the North and the South of the country, the difference in terrain between the East and West—from the Atlantic to the Pacific—is quite pronounced.

The country's big northeastern cities are New York, Boston, Baltimore, Philadelphia, and the capital of the country, Washington, D.C. This region is where the first **colonists** from Europe landed after crossing the Atlantic Ocean. Very urbanized, but still well forested, this part of industrial America is home to one American in five. Farther to the south, Virginia is known for tobacco farming, Louisiana for jazz, and Florida for its coastal resorts and citrus growing.

The Midwest extends over the center of the continental United States, its wide open prairie country—the Great Plains—covered with vast fields of wheat, corn, and soybeans. The Mississippi River cuts America in half from north to south, from Chicago and the Great Lakes area to the huge pastures and oilfields of Texas, on the shores of the Gulf of Mexico.

In the American West—the Far West—we find a legendary region made up of immense plateaus, often desert country, and separated from one end to the other by the formidable wall of the Rocky Mountains. The **pioneers** waited until the end of the nineteenth century to make their way through the sometimes arid, sometimes icebound passes and settle on the Pacific shore, in California, over 3,000 miles (5,000 km) from their starting point, discovering incredible sites of natural beauty on their way. Today, western cities have large populations and Los Angeles, with more than 30 million inhabitants, ranks first in the country in population!

Left: The Colorado River
Right: The New York City skyline

WHO DISCOVERED AMERICA?

Five hundred years ago, Christopher Columbus, a Genovese sailor in the service of the king and queen of Spain, landed in what is now America. Viking navigators are believed to have approached the same coasts four centuries earlier; but "Indians" who met Columbus when he landed where the first inhabitants of America.

A rriving from Siberia over 10,000 years ago, when the Bering Strait was dry enough to be walked across, the Indians migrated from Alaska to the pampas of Patagonia in present-day Argentina, by way of the North American plains, Mexico, the Amazonian forests, and the Andes, which was the territory of the **Incan** empire.

It was **Christopher Columbus** who discovered America in 1492, but it was to be **Amerigo Vespucci,** a minor explorer who had served under Columbus, for whom the land would be named.

When the leaders of overpopulated Europe discovered the wealth of the American continent, they were anxious to colonize. Spain, in the wake of Columbus' voyages, rushed into the conquest of Central America and Peru, destroying existing civilizations while pillaging the riches belonging to the Indians and enslaving them.

It wasn't long before other European countries followed suit, launching fleets into the conquest of what was then known as the New World. Portugal colonized present-day Brazil, France gave its king's name to the territory of Louisiana, and took Canada. On the east coast, England and Holland set up trading posts from which hunters and trappers set out in quest of furs.

Around 1600, hoards of European colonists arrived. They then brought in slaves from Africa to clear and farm the land that had belonged to the Indians. Thus, the Indians were forced off their land.

Top: Native American woman (Navajo)
Bottom Left: An Eskimo family
Bottom Right: Discovery of the New World (engraving)

HOW DID AMERICAN INDIANS LIVE IN THE PAST?

Before the European conquest, the Indians of North America were divided into a number of nations, each nation having its own lifestyle, closely attuned to the natural environment in the region where they lived.

In the far North, the Eskimos in Alaska lived near the sea from which they took their food. In winter they lived in dome-shaped houses called **igloos.** The forest dwellers—Algonquins, Iroquois, and Hurons—settled along the Atlantic coast and lived by hunting and gathering as well as farming, growing mainly squash, beans, and corn.

The prairie and hill Indians—Cheyenne, Blackfoot, and Sioux—moved with the changing seasons, hunting the great herds of buffalo that provided them with meat and with leather to make their clothes and build their tents, or **tepees.** In the Southwest, the Pueblo lived in amazing **troglodytic** villages, where they cultivated sweet potatoes or raised turkeys on the edges of a torrid desert, on the fringes of Apache and Navajo hunting grounds. West coast Indians lived off the fish they caught in the sea or the rivers. In the South, the Seminoles in Florida farmed, hunted, and fished. They lived in Everglades swamp villages in houses called **chickees.**

All these tribes, whose languages were as different as their lifestyles, occasionally engaged in ferocious wars with each other. Essentially, however, the Indians shared a common culture, based upon a deep-seated belief in the harmony of man and nature.

Left: A Native American celebration (Navajo)
Right: Troglodyte village

WHAT IS THE MEANING OF THE AMERICAN FLAG?

The 13 red and white stripes symbolize the 13 original American colonies that revolted against the British in 1776 to gain their independence. Today, there are 50 states in the United States, represented by the 50 white stars on a blue background.

The **Declaration of Independence**, signed in 1776, and later the **Constitution**, which the 13 original states adopted after the War of Independence, was influenced in part by the Magna Carta, John Locke, and the eighteenth-century philosophers Rousseau and Montesquieu. The concept of individual freedom and the hope of economic success as a result of the exploitation of vast virgin lands caused tens of millions of immigrants to come pouring into America, first from Europe, and later from all over the world.

After the first 13 colonies, most of the new states that joined the Union were founded by American colonists who were forced to go farther and farther west to settle. Some territories were purchased from the colonial powers: those in the Midwest from France, Florida from Spain, Alaska from Russia. Other were conquered by force: California and land in the Southwest were ceded to the United States by Mexico as a result of the Mexican War.

Although the United States is one nation, each state enjoys broad autonomy, particularly in legislative matters (for instance, some states have a death penalty, while others do not), educational policy, and taxation (state taxes vary with each state).

The government has three branches: executive (president and vice-president), legislative (Senate and House of Representatives), and judiciary (the Supreme Court). The seat of government is in Washington, D.C.

Top: The cavalry carrying the American flag
Bottom: Union soldiers carrying the American flag during the Civil War

WHAT WAS THE CONQUEST OF THE WEST?

Lured by dreams of riches or the desire to settle on still-virgin lands, large numbers of immigrants from all over the world were to take the westward trail and try the great adventure.

Much of what we know today about the epic of the Far West we have learned from the movies—westerns—through scenes that have become classics: pioneers struggling to survive on the rugged terrain, wars with Indians, **stagecoaches** being attacked by Indians or outlaws, and so on. The reality was probably less romantic but just as harsh. For two centuries, thousands of people fled their countries, some from rural poverty, some from religious persecution, and some from the sordid conditions in the industrial cities, toward this land of hope and freedom.

After landing in New York, many immigrants settled in urban areas. If they were interested in traveling westward, however, and if they had the money to buy supplies, they joined a group of pioneers and traveled by covered wagon.

After a long, dangerous journey, they reached a destination where they would clear the land, build houses, schools, churches, stores, and saloons, and keep order through the authority of an elected sheriff.

Memories of the hardships they had endured provided the basis for the famous "pioneer spirit"—a blend of daring, tenacity, and the hope of finding a better life. This unquestionably led to the birth of the spirit of enterprise found in present-day Americans, in industry, finance, scientific research, and countless other areas.

Top: Native Americans in Monument Valley, Utah
Bottom: A stagecoach in the Old West

WHEN WAS THE FIRST GOLD RUSH?

Gold has always exerted a powerful influence over human beings. Its discovery had led to wealth and power. Unfortunately, however, the possession of gold does not necessarily contribute to happiness.

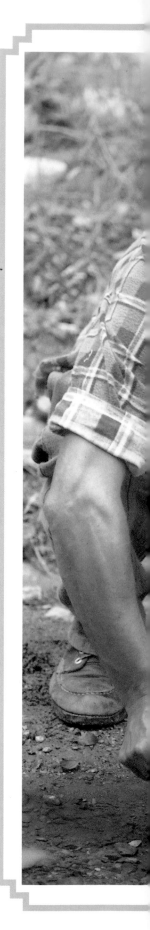

The first gold rush began in California in 1849 after the discovery of gold nuggets in a stream at Sutter's Mill. The news quickly spread, even as far away as Europe. Countless numbers of people made their way across the Atlantic and across the country, convinced they would make their fortunes in a land where gold was to be picked up like pebbles. **Prospectors** bringing all types of equipment rushed to the gold fields and set up camp. Some rich deposits were found, but most of the prospectors were not successful.

In 1859, the discovery in western Nevada of a new vein known as the Comstock Lode led to another gold rush. As soon as the prospectors found a few ounces of gold, their camp became a tent city. When the vein turned out to be a rich one, the first tradesmen arrived and rough wooden houses were put up. Twenty years later, when the vein was exhausted, the town was abandoned, and became a ghost town.

Gold discovered in Nome, Alaska, in 1898 and Fairbanks in 1902 attracted so many eager people that the population of Alaska doubled in ten years. Today the prospector, armed with his pick and accompanied by his donkey, is a romantic, somewhat traditional image. The gold fields are owned by mining companies, and geologists and professional miners do the extracting. Gold, now quoted on the stock market, is subject to profitability criteria controlled by the businessmen who manage its production. So the era of the "adventurers" in that area has come to an end.

Left: A goldminer
Right: A gold nugget

ARE THERE STILL COWBOYS?

The cowboys' main job is to guard herds of cattle. They ride their horses over the vast expanses where the cattle roam and live.

Western movies have made the cowboy a romantic, legendary character, forever battling cattle rustlers and fierce Indians who are attempting to defend their hunting grounds.

Today, the huge herds of cattle browse peacefully and the cowboys have put away their guns. They no longer ride herd at full gallop. Instead, cars and even helicopters have taken the place of horses for watching over the land and cattle on the ranches.

The atmosphere of the Old West is still present in small western and southwestern towns when the big cattle sales take place. **Rodeos** are held in which competing cowboys show their strength and skill. Their prowess is inspired by their work: calf roping, bull riding, steer wrestling; and bronco riding.

Left: A re-creation of an Old Western town
Bottom: A bucking bronco in a rodeo

24

WHAT WERE THE CAUSES OF THE CIVIL WAR?

While the Northeast of the United States quickly became a modern industrial area, the South remained primarily an agricultural region where a few rich planters prospered as a result of the labor of their slaves.

BOOM

It was as much for economic reasons as for moral ones that America was torn apart during the Civil War. In 1860 Abraham Lincoln was elected president on an antislavery platform. The Confederate (Southern) states, determined to hold on to their traditional way of life that depended on the existence of slavery, seceded from the Union, thus beginning the Civil War, which tore the country apart for four bloody years. In 1863 Lincoln's **Emancipation Proclamation** declared that slaves would be free. In April, 1865, Southern General Robert E. Lee surrendered to Northern General Ulysses S. Grant and the Civil War ended. Lincoln was shot by John Wilkes Booth while attending the theater. He died the following day. The Thirteenth Amendment to the Constitution abolishing slavery went into effect later that year.

Even though the African American community, which today makes up almost 15 percent of the population of the United States, was thus able to emerge from slavery, it did not thereby succeed in freeing itself from poverty or racial discrimination. In the South, **racism** and hate groups like the Ku Klux Klan have not completely died out, and **ghettos** that are often crime-infested slums exist in all large American cities. Many African Americans have risen to positions of power in local, state, and federal government, and their voices are being heard throughout the country in every area: politics, the judiciary, business, education, literature, the performing arts, and so on.

A re-creation of a Civil War battle

WHAT ARE THE ORIGINS OF JAZZ?

Blending the rhythms of their native Africa with the traditional music of the colonists from Europe, black slaves brought to the New World the musical bases of jazz.

Beginning in the seventeenth century, blacks from Africa, transported by the millions in the holds of slave-trading vessels, provided the agricultural manpower on the huge cotton plantations in the South. Bought, sold, and put to work, they were fed, cared for, and often mistreated by their owners. Although some of them became house servants, most of the slaves worked in the fields. The life they led was rigorous and bitter. Their music provided some comfort as they toiled, and homesickness for their native Africa comes through in the rhythms that they devised and in interpreting for themselves the various kinds of music from Europe. Thus were created gospel, adapted from hymns, and blues, which came out of old ballads from Ireland and England.

Beginning in the early 1900s in the nightclubs of Storyville in New Orleans, and on the Mississippi **showboats,** there was to be an explosion of ragtime and jazz. Eventually, the sound reached Chicago and New York. The 1920s was the Golden Age of Jazz, and these diverse musical trends gave rise to the rock music played and listened to today all over the world.

New Orleans jazz musicians

WHO ARE THE AMERICANS?

The 240 million Americans whose ancestors came from all over the world make up a diverse society...without giving up their cultural identity in the process.

The first waves of immigrants were mainly composed of Irish, Scottish, and English colonists, whose language was adopted by the new country. There were also people from Holland, Germany, and Sweden. A century later, Italians, Greeks, Poles, Russians, as well as Chinese, Jews from all countries, and Armenians arrived on the shores of the new land.

Today, in addition to a sizeable African American population, the United States is also home to a very large Spanish-speaking group. Besides the colonists long established in Texas and California, it includes more recent immigrants from Mexico, Cuba, and Puerto Rico. Numbering some twenty million, this population has made Spanish the second most important language in the country.

Living side by side and holding on to their traditions, the various ethnic communities form an astonishing mosaic. New York, for instance, has a large population of African Americans, Puerto Ricans, Asians, and Jews from all over the world; Los Angeles and San Francisco have large Mexican and Asian communities; German immigrants settled in Pennsylvania and the Midwest; Boston has a large Irish population; and so on. While observing their own religious or ethnic holidays, these various groups also participate in national holidays, such as Thanksgiving Day in November and the Fourth of July.

Some typical American faces

WHAT DOES THE STATUE OF LIBERTY REPRESENT?

A gift from France, the huge statue has stood since 1886 at the entrance to New York harbor. It symbolizes "Liberty bringing light to the world," and has greeted immigrants from all over the world coming to find a new and better life.

The Statue of Liberty, now a national monument, is one of the major symbols of human rights and equal opportunity. Indeed, this symbol, along with the Four Freedoms—freedom from want, freedom from fear, freedom of worship, and, of course, freedom of speech—forms the basis of the American ideal. The power of information via television and newspapers cannot be underestimated. The media—radio, television, newspapers, magazines—play an important role in influencing public opinion, and all Americans are free to express themselves.

As everywhere else, there is often a big gap between the ideal and the reality. Although the basic rights of citizens are respected, social inequalities are still present. Racism and poverty still exist and the government must concern itself with helping the disadvantaged, the poor, the unemployed, and the homeless.

The United States faces major problems: crime, drug and alcohol abuse, homelessness, poverty, the **AIDS** epidemic, the need for health care reform, overpopulation, pollution, and so on. It is hoped that with new legislation and a great deal of money, some of these problems will eventually be alleviated.

The Statue of Liberty

WHO WAS THE FIRST PRESIDENT OF THE UNITED STATES?

Washington, the capital of the United States, owes its name to George Washington, the first president, elected in 1789. Today, the president lives and works in the White House at 1600 Pennsylvania Avenue.

Presidential elections are held every four years. First, the major political parties—Democrat and Republican—hold conventions at which they nominate a candidate for president and vice-president. Then the candidates travel across the country, giving speeches about their platform (what they believe and what they plan to do if elected). Elections are held the first Tuesday after the first Monday in November, and the new executives are inaugurated on January 20. In 1993 Democrat William Jefferson Clinton became the forty-second president of the United States.

After the Great Depression of the 1930s, the United States gradually abandoned an isolationist policy toward Europe. In 1941, after the Japanese attack on Pearl Harbor, it entered the Second World War and contributed to the victory of the **Allies** in 1945. Afterward, it participated broadly in reconstruction of the war-ravaged countries through the **Marshall Plan.** Then Americans began the fight against communism in the four corners of the earth; cold war against the USSR, war in Korea and then in Vietnam. Relations between the White House and the **Kremlin** nevertheless improved gradually, and permitted atomic weapons limitation between the two superpowers. Since the recent dissolution of the Eastern Bloc and the former USSR, the United States of America is more than ever the most influential country in the world, in terms of both economics and politics.

Left: A ticker tape parade on
      Fifth Avenue in New York City
Right: The White House

IS THE DOLLAR STILL STRONG?

The top economic power in the world, the United States first became powerful because of its underground natural resources (coal, oil, and various minerals), its agricultural production, and various industries.

One of the main characteristics of the United States is the vitality of its business world. Free enterprise has fostered the creation of thousands of companies, sometimes managed by self-made men who started from scratch and built up economic empires, such as that of Rockefeller in oil, Ford in automobiles, or Carnegie, the Scot who arrived in the United States penniless at the age of 12 and became one of the richest men in the world, controlling dozens of steelworks. These often colorful characters make up part of the American legend as models of social success.

The American currency, the dollar, having become the international reference currency, has for half a century symbolized the economic power of the United States. The slightest change in the dollar rate affects all the stock markets in the world. In recent years, however, the American balance of trade has become negative as the United States buys more than it sells. In addition, the competition of Germany and, in particular, Japan, affects the health of the giant American automotive and international electronics corporations, such as General Motors and IBM.

Top: Oil wells
Bottom: American money

WHY IS AMERICA "THE WORLD'S STOREHOUSE"?

With the Corn Belt, an area specializing in growing corn and soybeans, and the Wheat Belt, with its huge wheat fields, the Midwest has become one of the world's largest agricultural producers.

Despite its obvious resources and heavy industrialization, American farming is in crisis. Faced with competition from Australia, Canada, and the European Community (the EEC), producers in the Midwest are having trouble selling their products. Small family farms are gradually disappearing, bought out by large **agribusiness** companies managing oversized fields that are artificially irrigated and furrowed by sophisticated farming machinery.

California and Florida produce an abundance of vegetables and citrus fruit, such as oranges, lemons, and grapefruit. California also has many highly developed, successful vineyards. The island of Hawaii is famed for its sugarcane and pineapple plantations, as well as coffee and nuts. Cotton and tobacco are grown in the southern states, Idaho is known for its potatoes, and apples grow plentifully in Washington State and New York. Alaska is known for its fish industry.

Even though the cowboys have become tame, cattle raising is still a very important activity. Americans, however, have cut back on the consumption of beef. Dairy products from the Milk Belt in the northern Great Plains and around the Great Lakes are consumed in quantity.

Top: Cotton growing in the south
Bottom: Wheat harvest in the midwest

WHAT DO AMERICANS EAT?

In recent years, Americans have begun to pay a great deal of attention to the benefits of a balanced diet and don't live exclusively on hamburgers washed down with huge quantities of soft drinks....

A typical American breakfast consists of fruit juice, hot or cold cereal, and toast, or eggs with bacon or ham, or pancakes with syrup, all accompanied by milk, coffee, or tea. Lunch is usually a fast meal: a salad, sandwich, hamburger, or yogurt, again with coffee or tea or a soft drink.

Dinner is usually the large meal of the day. It might consist of beef, chicken, or fish. Potatoes or rice, vegetables, and salad often accompany the main dish, and sometimes bread or dinner rolls are added, followed by dessert—cake, pie, pudding, ice cream, or fruit. Lately, various types of pasta dishes have become extremely popular.

Each region of the United States has its specialties. The South is known for its fried chicken and biscuits with gravy. Westerners eat steak and chile—the hotter the better. Californians love their salad bars and Mexican food, such as tacos and tortillas. In New Orleans, Creole dishes with rice, fish, and shellfish are popular. Boston is also known for seafood (as well as beans), and Maine lobster is world famous. Many immigrants brought their recipes with them long ago and now, from one end of the country to the other, there are Italian pizzerias and Chinese, Greek, French, Indian, Thai, and Japanese restaurants that give the country astonishing gastronomic variety.

Typical American food

HOW DO PEOPLE GET AROUND IN THE UNITED STATES?

Cars, buses, trains, and airplanes are on the move all the time throughout America today. But when the first colonists landed, there was no way to move from place to place except on the rivers and along the Indian trails....

The Americans' biggest task in the nineteenth century was to link together areas as far apart as the Atlantic and Pacific coasts, by crossing the vast virgin lands in the middle of the continent. Today we have the world's foremost transport system: almost 4 million miles (6.3 million km) of roads, and over 47,000 miles (77,000 km) of freeways carrying heavy traffic.

One can travel for days on the panoramic highways, admiring the scenery along the way behind the wheel of a car or in an air-conditioned bus. The big cities have freeways that enable people to get to work, drop their children off at school, or do their shopping, often a very long way from their homes. In sprawling cities such as Los Angeles, most people do not walk but use automobiles to get everywhere. In large metropolitan cities such as New York and Boston, people travel underground in subways. Although often crowded and not very clean, they are still the fastest and most practical way to get around in large cities.

Although 75 percent of all American rail passengers ride commuter trains, such as the Long Island Railroad, thus relieving rush hour traffic jams and helping to conserve fuel, railroads today are used mainly for transporting goods.

When it's necessary to travel long distances, Americans prefer to fly, whether it's for business, to take a vacation, or to visit relatives. In many isolated areas, a small private plane or a helicopter is the only way to get to the nearest town or to school, or even to get to the neighbors' house for a drink before dinner...

Left: A superhighway
Right: A private airplane

WHAT DO AMERICANS DRIVE?

The automobile is a vital part of American life, and an integral part of the landscape in America.

In a country as vast as America, for work or for recreation, the car is the all-important means of travel. Since a driver may spend the greater part of the day behind the wheel, life is organized around the roads. There are service stations, motels, and drive-ins everywhere: banks, restaurants, and even religious services where you go in by car....

The automobile has a long history in the United States. In 1908, while in Europe only motor carriages were being built for a clientele of aristocrats, Henry Ford invented the car that was to bear his name—the Ford "Model T"—a production line car, mass-produced, serviceable, and affordable. Within a few short years, the city of Detroit became the heart of an enormous automobile industry, producing ever more modern cars with famous trademarks: Cadillac, Chevrolet, Chrysler.

Today, large automobiles, which are heavy fuel consumers, are suffering from the competition of the more compact and economical Japanese cars, and more and more Americans drive small cars. With this in mind, the American automobile industry has developed compact cars, such as the Chevrolet Cavalier, the Plymouth Sundance, and the Ford Escort.

Cars and trucks

WHY IS AMERICA THE LAND OF THE SKYSCRAPER?

Oddly enough, this country with its wide open spaces is the one most concerned about saving space by constructing ever taller buildings.

The skyscrapers that rise in the centers of American cities count their stories by the dozen. There is some living space in them, but usually they house the offices of large businesses employing thousands of people. In fact, as they vied for prestige at the end of the nineteenth century, businessmen in New York and Chicago began building higher and higher towers.

The Empire State Building in New York, with its height of 1,250 feet (381 m) remained the tallest building for a long time. Then this skyscraper lost its title to the twin towers of the World Trade Center, constructed at the end of Manhattan and rising to 1,350 feet (411 m). Today the record is held by the Sears Tower in Chicago: 110 floors and 1,440 feet (443 m) high!

Such competition encourages every large city to build the skyscraper that will outdistance all the others. Thus, all the business centers have their characteristic skylines, recognizable from afar by the outlines of a few famous buildings: New York, Boston, Seattle, St. Louis….

New York City

WHO WERE AL CAPONE AND THE UNTOUCHABLES?

Al Capone and his rival Bugs Moran were the heads of the two main criminal organizations that became wealthy through contraband alcohol and racketeering. It all took place in Chicago, during the Prohibition era....

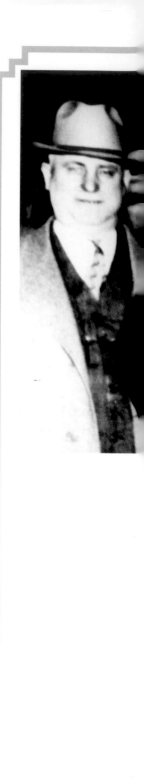

In the 1920s, **Prohibition** (under which the sale of alcohol was forbidden) gave rise to large-scale alcohol trafficking and crime. The Chicago underworld took advantage of Prohibition to establish its power, "buying" police officials and shady politicians in order to avoid prosecution. Having become almost unassailable as a result of the corruption of local authorities, the gangsters carried on a bloody war among themselves in broad daylight. In Chicago, it was like being caught up in the worst moments of the Wild West!

The "Untouchables"—members of the FBI—worked to restore order. It took them years to arrest the hundreds of gangsters involved in murder and other crimes.

Today the FBI is still fighting organized crime. They are also involved in attempting to halt drug trafficking, which has become a major problem in the United States. **Cartels** from Asia and Colombia, South America, are known to be responsible for bringing drugs into the United States, and the use of "crack" cocaine and heroin has escalated, leading to a rise in crime throughout the country.

Top: Gangster Al Capone
Bottom: California Highway Patrol

HOW MANY TELEVISION NETWORKS ARE THERE IN THE UNITED STATES?

There are over 1,000 television networks in the United States—and Americans spend an average of seven hours a day in front of the small screen!

In the past, newly arrived immigrants got to know about their new country through the press. Perhaps that tradition is at the bottom of the American passion for news. Today, in addition to television, there are 9,000 newspapers and 11,000 magazines in the United States....

Television schedules earmark a lot of time for news and sports, as well as for dramas, "sitcoms," and soap operas, in which there appear characters that set America to dreaming: men and women vying for success and prestige, often living in luxury. Thus, there are added to the traditional values of the various communities in the country some of the grand ideals of the "American dream": adventure, aspiration to personal success and happiness, and the struggle against the forces of evil.

Some specialized networks devote all their programs to news, as does the famous CNN; others are devoted to music (MTV), to sports for the sports-crazy American public, or even to religion. The latter networks belong to one of the countless religious communities that flourish in the United States, protected by freedom of worship. Many immigrants who arrived in the past were fleeing from religious persecution, as, for example, the Jews from Russia and Germany, Catholics from Ireland and Scotland, Protestants from France or Germany, and Christian sects such as the Mormons, Quakers, and Amish.

CNN television studio

22

HOW DID THE AMERICAN MOVIE INDUSTRY START?

Hundreds of movie heroes were created in the famous studios in Hollywood, California, the capital of the American movie industry since 1920....

Although movie-making was invented in France by the Lumiere brothers, it was in the United States that it became a popular art. Silent films introduced such popular stars as the great Charlie Chaplin, Mary Pickford, Douglas Fairbanks, and Rudolph Valentino. The first full-length talking picture was The Jazz Singer in 1927... and the Hollywood "dream factory" was born.

Studios such as Metro-Goldwyn-Mayer, Paramount, Columbia, and Warner Brothers produced all sorts of films—westerns, sentimental epics, detective films, science fiction, and musicals. Famous stars included Clark Gable, Humphrey Bogart, Lana Turner, Fred Astaire, and Ginger Rogers. Expensive films like Gone With The Wind had huge audiences, grossed a great deal of money, and won many Academy Awards, also called Oscars. More recent "block-busters" include E.T. the Extra-Terrestrial (1982) and Jurassic Park (1993).

If the United States seems so familiar to people in other countries, it is largely due to American movies and music. With worldwide distribution, the movies have made it possible for thousands of spectators to travel a dream America without getting out of their seats!

Top: Making a western movie
Bottom Left: "Jaws" at Universal Studios, Hollywood
Bottom Right: A scene from Gone With The Wind

23

WHO ARE TINTIN'S AMERICAN COUSINS?

Tintin has more cousins in the United States than anywhere else. They are found not only in comic strips but on screen as well, thanks to animated cartoons by the grand master of the genre: Walt Disney.

W alt Disney is the most famous American cartoonist, of course. His characters, Mickey Mouse, Donald Duck, Goofy, Pluto, and others have traveled the world. He was also an animator of genius. *Snow White and the Seven Dwarfs*, made in 1938, was his first full-length animated feature. It was such a success in the United States and in the entire world that the Disney studios in Hollywood have become a gigantic business employing thousands of artists and movie makers, creating countless movies for both screen and television, and reviving the characters in a book publishing business of its own.

In 1955 Walt Disney Enterprises opened Disneyland, near Los Angeles. Its enchanting settings, rides, and shows have made it the model for theme parks worldwide. A second park, Walt Disney World, opened in Florida in 1971 and receives over 20 million visitors a year, while the one in Tokyo has been equally successful since 1983. The fourth giant park, Euro Disney, opened in 1992 near Paris, France.

Tintin's American counterparts are not all charming little characters; from yesterday's heroes, like Superman or Batman, to today's Ninja Turtles, to say nothing of the heroes of western-style or detective comic strips, the world of cartoon fiction in the United States is as varied as the American population itself.

The Magic Kingdom at Disneyland: Pinocchio entertains some children

24

WHO WALKED ON THE MOON?

For a long time the United States and the former Soviet Union were rivals in the race to conquer space....

During the cold war years, the two world super-powers, the United States and the Soviet Union, entered the space race, with the conquest of the moon as the objective. The former USSR took an early lead with the 1957 launching into orbit of *Sputnik*, the first unmanned satellite. Later, *Sputnik* carried a dog on board, and finally, in 1961, a man, cosmonaut Yuri Gagarin, traveled into space.

In the years that followed, the two powers took turns improving the record for time spent in space. Then on July 20, 1969, NASA, the American organization in charge of space travel and research, scored decisively by realizing an old dream as Jules Verne had already imag-ined it: having a man walk on the moon. The Apollo 11 mission, observed throughout the world by means of tele-vision, showed astronaut Neil Armstrong setting foot on the surface of the moon for the first time.

In 1981 a space shuttle was built that was the first manned spacecraft designed to be reused. Space medi-cine was developed to study the problems of living and working in space. Today, satellites are used for telecom-munications, to help navigate ships, and to help leaders of scientific expeditions and search and rescue opera-tions. In 1988 an agreement was signed between the United States, Canada, Japan, and nine members of the European Space Agency to set up an international space station in the mid- to late 1990s.

Left: Space shuttle launch from Kennedy Space Center, Florida
Right: Astronaut Neil Armstrong walks on the moon

25

DO PEOPLE STILL HUNT BUFFALO?

The buffalo was driven to near-extinction by hunting and changes made to its natural habitat. Today, wild animals are protected in large conservation parks.

The American prairies were once home to millions of buffalo. The big, thick-fleeced ruminant weighed almost a ton. Originally, the Indians hunted them on foot with bows and spears. Later, they hunted on horseback. Before the arrival of the Spanish, the Indians were unfamiliar with horses and, instead, used dogs as pack animals. When a few runaway horses ran wild, the Indians captured them and tamed them for their use. The Comanche would later call these horses "sacred dogs."

The buffalo provided the Indians with meat and with leather for their clothing and tents, but they and the American pioneers slaughtered them in such numbers, at first for food and later for the mere pleasure of hunting them, that by 1809 there were only 551 buffalo left in the entire American territory. The species was almost extinct by the time it was rescued by the creation of the national parks.

Many species of animals are found only in North America: the caribou, the wapiti deer, the dangerous grizzly bear, the puma, the coyote, and the mountain goat, among others. The bald eagle is the national bird and is protected by an Act of Congress. Plant life is also very varied. In the deserts of Arizona and New Mexico are many types of **cactus** plants. The world's largest and most ancient tree is the sequoia, a conifer found in the forests of California that may grow to a height of 500 feet (150 m) or more and live for 2,000 years.

Top: Buffalo in Yellowstone National Park, Wyoming
Bottom: Musk oxen in Alaska

26

WHAT IS THE LIFE OF NATIVE AMERICANS LIKE TODAY?

The Native Americans, outsiders in their native land since the conquest of the West, became impoverished and discouraged. Today they have rediscovered their traditions and take great pride in their origins.

The last attempt of the Native Americans at resistance ended in 1890 at the Battle of Wounded Knee, in South Dakota, with the massacre of the Sioux. The survivors were confined to **reservations,** lands that were often vast but infertile and worthless. Demoralized by the loss of what had been its sources of pride—freedom, wide open spaces, and traditions—the Native Americans gradually grew weaker. Before long, only a quarter of a million were left.

Today, many Native Americans live in large cities. The Kahnawake, for instance, who are not bothered by heights, provide a work force that is highly valued by skyscraper builders. Others continue to farm their land, while still others make a living by designing and selling jewelry, native art, and crafts to tourists. Some, like the Navajo, have been very successful in exploiting the oil beneath their land, then investing the profits in irrigating and farming the previously desert-like land.

At the beginning of the 1970s, the Native Americans secured restitution of some lands and the right to resume the practice of their ancestral religion. Today, one and one-half million Native Americans are gradually rediscovering their true identity and preserving their traditions within the modern world.

Left: Native American at "totem pole" in Monument Valley, Utah
Right: Native Americans at the entrance to their home in Monument Valley

27

WHY WERE NATIONAL PARKS CREATED?

Impressed by the great beauty of the places they discovered as they explored the country, Americans began to want to protect those places from human interference.

Y ellowstone National Park in Wyoming, founded in 1872, is the nation's oldest national park. The United States now has about 50 natural parks. Each park has its own natural points of interest, such as the 200 geysers (Old Faithful is the most spectacular), hot springs, and volcanic mud pools in Yellowstone National Park, the world's largest caverns in Carlsbad National Park in New Mexico, active volcanoes in Hawaii, the Painted Desert containing the Petrified Forest in Arizona, and the awesome vistas of the Grand Canyon, also in Arizona.

Other parks contain many more natural treasures: a tropical swamp filled with wildlife in the Florida Everglades, majestic redwoods in California, or simply splendid lake and forest landscapes. The most recently created parks are located—Mount McKinley, which rises to over 19,500 ft (6,000 m)—as well as superb glaciers and polar areas. All these landscapes are preserved from the ill effects of pollution resulting from human activity.

One of the most touching of the historical parks is Mesa Verde, in Colorado, which contains the ruins of hundreds of grottoes and villages built by Indians over a period of more than 1,000 years. These are the vestiges of one of the oldest of the American civilizations.

Top: The Rocky Mountains
Bottom Left: A young bear in Yellowstone National Park
Bottom Right: A sign for Sequoia National Park, California

28

WHAT ARE THE GREAT RIVERS OF NORTH AMERICA?

The Mississippi—which the Indians called the "Father of Waters"—with its great tributary, the Missouri, is one of the longest rivers in the world.

The Mississippi, about 2,340 miles (3,766 km) long, crosses the United States from North to South and is an important channel of communications. In the nineteenth century it was traveled by hundreds of steam-driven flat-bottomed vessels (the river is shallow in places) propelled by paddle wheels. These steamboats carried the cotton and sugar produced in the South to the factories in the North, and returned loaded with cereals and meat. Veritable floating palaces, the **showboats** offered luxurious cabins and gambling casinos to businessmen traveling between New Orleans, Memphis, and St. Louis, the great ports erected along the banks of the river.

This picturesque world all but disappeared upon the arrival of the railroad, but the Mississippi still carries many barges loaded with timber or coal, and you can still ride a showboat or two. In addition to the Missouri, its principle tributaries are the Ohio and the Arkansas, which it encounters before emptying, at the end of its course, into the Gulf of Mexico.

Other major rivers are the Rio Grande, or Large River, 1,885 miles (3,034 km), which marks the border between the United States and Mexico, and the Colorado, or the Red River, 1,450 miles (2,333 km) long. Without the plentiful waters of the Colorado River, life would be impossible in the dry American West. There is also the Yukon, 1,979 miles (3,185 km) long, which flows across the polar expanses of Alaska. Icebound a large portion of the year, it is rarely used for navigation.

Left: The Colorado River
in the Grand Canyon
Right: A Mississippi riverboat

29

WHAT IS THE GRAND CANYON?

The Grand Canyon of the Colorado is considered to be one of the great natural wonders of the world. For 277 miles (446 km) the Colorado River has hollowed out a ravine that is up to 1 mile (1.6 km) deep in places.

The Colorado River, a modest sort of watercourse at first, rises in the Rocky Mountains, in the state of Colorado. Flowing more freely by the time it enters Utah, it is soon joined by the Green River, whose torrential waters have already flowed through the deep canyons of the Lodore. Thus, it is a mighty river that approaches the gorges of the Grand Canyon. It has taken the Colorado River millions of years, with the help of wind and freezing temperatures, to hollow out this ravine in the rock. A veritable open-air museum, sculpted in red and white sandstone, the Grand Canyon shelters dinosaur remains and fossils. There are also many kinds of animals and plants there that are very much alive: **iguanas**, rattlesnakes, scorpions, desert cactuses, and pine forests swarming with squirrels.

Grand Canyon National Park receives more than three million visitors every year. One can travel the area by train, by car or by tour bus, climb down the cliffs on foot or on a mule, be bounced around on a raft by the tumultuous waters of the river, or fly over the canyon in a helicopter.

Not far from this awesome landscape, you can visit the castles hollowed out by a runoff on a slope of multicolored rock in Bryce Canyon, the natural bridges sculpted by the wind in Arches Park, a petrified forest, or even the oddly shaped mountains in Zion Park. All these geological wonders are concentrated within the territory of three of the fifty states: Arizona, Colorado, and Utah.

Top: A double arch at Arches National Park, Utah
Bottom: The Grand Canyon

30

WHICH SPORTS DO AMERICANS LIKE BEST?

From skiing to rafting, from surfing to golf, skateboarding, or jogging, Americans enjoy sports and live in a country that encourages participation in many.

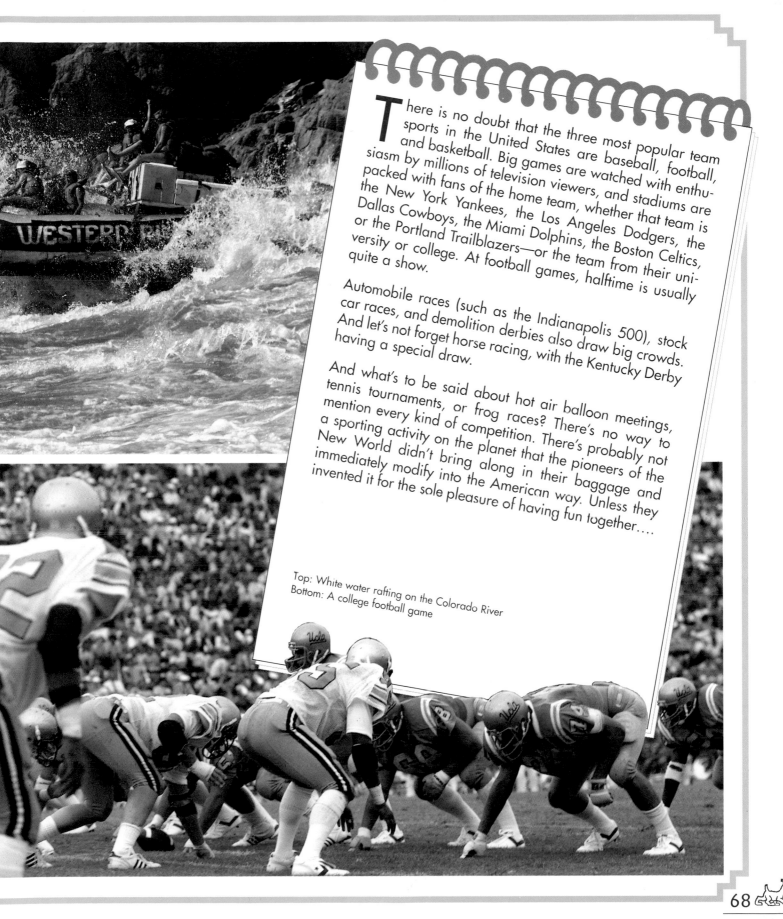

There is no doubt that the three most popular team sports in the United States are baseball, football, and basketball. Big games are watched with enthusiasm by millions of television viewers, and stadiums are packed with fans of the home team, whether that team is the New York Yankees, the Los Angeles Dodgers, the Dallas Cowboys, the Miami Dolphins, the Boston Celtics, or the Portland Trailblazers—or the team from their university or college. At football games, halftime is usually quite a show.

Automobile races (such as the Indianapolis 500), stock car races, and demolition derbies also draw big crowds. And let's not forget horse racing, with the Kentucky Derby having a special draw.

And what's to be said about hot air balloon meetings, tennis tournaments, or frog races? There's no way to mention every kind of competition. There's probably not a sporting activity on the planet that the pioneers of the New World didn't bring along in their baggage and immediately modify into the American way. Unless they invented it for the sole pleasure of having fun together....

Top: White water rafting on the Colorado River
Bottom: A college football game

A

AGRIBUSINESS : industries that produce, distribute, and sell farm products.

AIDS : disorder caused by the HIV virus that results in the inability of the body to fight disease; first identified in 1981, it has become a worldwide epidemic, causing many deaths.

ALLIES : the countries that fought against Germany during the World Wars of the twentieth century: primarily, England, France, Russia, and the United States.

ALLIGATOR : from the Spanish *el legarto,* the lizard; crocodile-like reptile capable of growing to lengths of about 16 feet (5 m); common in the swamps of Florida and Louisiana.

ARCHIPELAGO : group of islands, such as the Hawaiian Islands.

C

CACTUS : plant found in dry regions that contains sharp, prickly spines instead of leaves.

CARTEL : commercial enterprises, often international, that are actually monopolies.

CHICKEE : Seminole Indian houses in the Florida Everglades; built three feet off the ground with palm leaf roofs.

COLD WAR : intense rivalry between the USSR (and, consequently, its communist allies) and the United States (and its Western allies); ended in 1991 with the dissolution of the Soviet Union.

COLONIST : person who leaves one country to establish a home in another.

COLUMBUS, CHRISTOPHER (1451–1506) : Italian navigator who, in the service of Spain, "discovered" America, believing he had reached the Indian subcontinent.

CONFEDERATE : member of a federation; in the Civil War the group of Southern states that seceded from the Union.

CONSTITUTION : basic principles and laws that determine the form of a country's government.

D

DECLARATION OF INDEPENDENCE : adopted in 1776 by the original 13 colonies, it states that people have certain inalienable rights to "life, liberty, and the pursuit of happiness," and that, if these rights are violated by the government, the people have the right to change the government.

E

EMANCIPATION PROCLAMATION : announcement by Abraham Lincoln in 1863 that slaves would be freed in the Southern states that were fighting against the North during the Civil War.

G

GEYSER : intermittently gushing spring of hot water; Old Faithful spurts every hour in Yellowstone National Park.

GHETTO : place where a community lives isolated from the rest of the population.

I

IGLOO : dome-shaped snowhouse lived in by the Eskimos of Alaska.

IGUANA : large tropical American lizard.

INCAN : pertaining to the empire of the Incas, Indians of Peru, Bolivia, and Ecuador, who were conquered by the Spanish.

K

KREMLIN : seat of the government of the former USSR; since December 1991, the seat of the Russian government.

M

MARSHALL PLAN : European reconstruction program proposed by George Marshall in 1947 for the countries of Western Europe. The American aid planned for four years (85 percent as a gift, 15 percent as long-term loans) was accompanied by a European political orientation for economic cooperation.

N

NUGGET : chunk of pure gold.

P

PIONEER : early settler who traveled westward to establish a new home.

PROHIBITION : a period during the 1920s when it was illegal to import, manufacture, or sell alcohol.

PROSPECTOR : in the middle of the late 1800s, one who searched for gold, primarily in the western United States.

R

RACISM : discrimination against members of a particular race.

RATTLESNAKE : highly venomous snake that has at the end of its tail a series of hollow cones producing a rattling sound.

RESERVATION : land on which Native Americans live.

RODEO : an exhibition and competition that comprises cowboy skills such as calf roping, bull riding, steer wrestling, and bronco riding.

S

SHOWBOAT : steamboat on the Mississippi River on which troups of actors gave performances for people living in communities along the river.

STAGECOACH : horse-drawn vehicle used in the Old West to transport passengers and mail.

T

TEPEE : cone-shaped Indian tent made of animal skins.

TROGLODYTE : inhabitant of a dwelling constructed inside a cave or a grotto.

V

VESPUCCI, AMERIGO (1451–1512) : Italian explorer who had sailed under Columbus in the service of Spain; he made four expeditions to the New World. In 1507 a German cartographer credited him with the discovery of the America continent that has borne his name ever since.

W

WESTERN : movie or story depicting life in the Old West.

WHITE HOUSE : Washington, D.C., residence and offices of the president of the United States; contains 132 rooms and covers 18 acres. It got its name because its polished white stone contrasted with the brick of neighboring buildings.

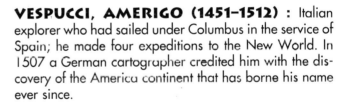

Chronology

BC

3000

The most ancient sculptures in North America are located on the coasts of Florida and Georgia (2500)

Founding of the capital city Memphis by Menes (3100)

2000

Beginning of the Olmec culture (c. 1200)

Bronze Age in Europe (1700 to 800)

1000

Hopewell culture in the forest regions of eastern North America (200)

First Olympic games (776)

0

Nazca hieroglyphs made (approx. 220)

End of the Western Roman Empire (476)

500

Decline of the Mayan culture (approx. 800)

Charlemagne crowned Emperor of the West, in Rome (800)

1000

Christopher Columbus discovers America (1492)

The Black Death kills more than 25 million people in Europe (1348–1350)

1500

The new continent is called America in honor of the Italian Amerigo Vespucci (1507)

The Reformation begins (1517)

1600

Founding of first permanent settlement in the New World at Jamestown (1607)

Rise of absolute monarchs: James I of England (1603–1625); Louis XIV of France (1643–1715)

1700

American Declaration of Independence (1776)

Union of England and Scotland under the name of Great Britain (1707)

1800

Importing of slaves into the United States prohibited (1807) American Civil War (1861–1865)

Karl Marx publishes the *Communist Manifesto* (1848)

1900

AD

Founding of United Nations in San Francisco (1945)

Atomic bombs dropped on Hiroshima and Nagasaki (1945)

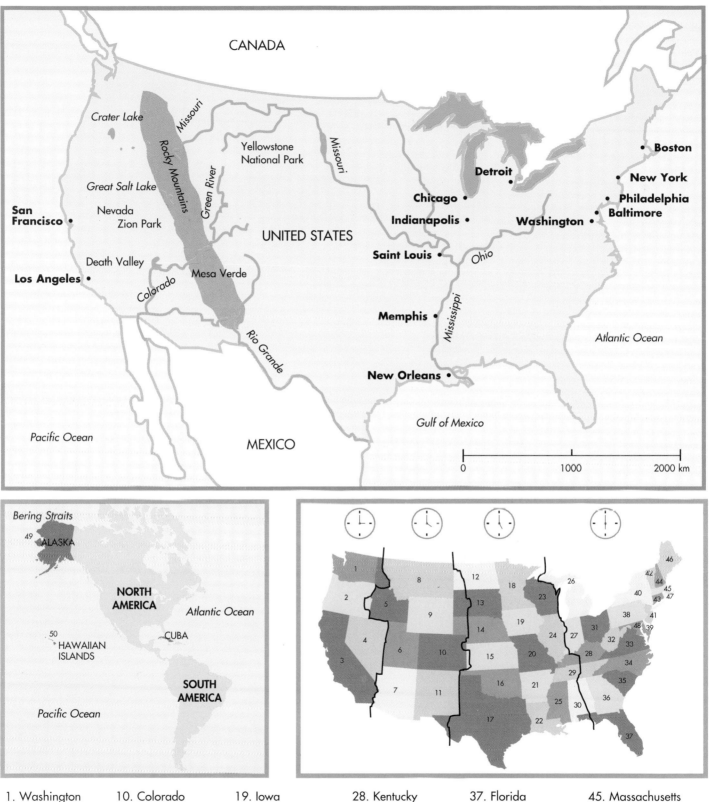

CANADA

Crater Lake

Missouri

Rocky Mountains

Green River

Yellowstone National Park

Missouri

• Boston

Detroit •

• New York

Chicago •

Great Salt Lake

Indianapolis •

• Philadelphia

San Francisco •

Nevada

Zion Park

UNITED STATES

Washington • • Baltimore

Death Valley

Saint Louis •

Ohio

Los Angeles •

Mesa Verde

Colorado

Memphis •

Mississippi

Atlantic Ocean

Rio Grande

New Orleans •

Pacific Ocean

MEXICO

Gulf of Mexico

0   1000   2000 km

Bering Straits

49 ALASKA

NORTH AMERICA

Atlantic Ocean

CUBA

50 HAWAIIAN ISLANDS

SOUTH AMERICA

Pacific Ocean

1. Washington	10. Colorado	19. Iowa	28. Kentucky	37. Florida	45. Massachusetts
2. Oregon	11. New Mexico	20. Missouri	29. Tennessee	38. Pennsylvania	46. Maine
3. California	12. North Dakota	21. Arkansas	30. Alabama	39. Delaware	47. Rhode Island
4. Nevada	13. South Dakota	22. Louisiana	31. Ohio	40. New York	48. Maryland +
5. Idaho	14. Nebraska	23. Wisconsin	32. West Virginia	41. New Jersey	District of
6. Utah	15. Kansas	24. Illinois	33. Virginia	42. Vermont	Columbia
7. Arizona	16. Oklahoma	25. Mississippi	34. North Carolina	43. Connecticut	49. Alaska
8. Montana	17. Texas	26. Michigan	35. South Carolina	44. New	50. Hawaii
9. Wyoming	18. Minnesota	27. Indiana	36. Georgia	Hampshire	

index

Anderson, Joan.
Christopher Columbus: From Vision to Voyage.
New York: Dial Books, 1991.

Davis, Mary.
From Walden Pond to Muirwoods: An Untraditional Travel Guide to the U.S.
Chicago: Noble Press, 1990.

Fradin, Dennis B.
California. Chicago:
Children's Press, 1992.

Goldman, Martin.
Nat Turner and the South Hampton Revolt of 1831. New York: F. Watts, 1992.

Grafton, John.
America: A History of the First 500 Years.
New York: Crescent Books, 1992.

Heth, Charlotte, editor.
Native American Dances, Ceremonies, and Social Traditions.
Washington, D.C.: Smithsonian Inst., 1992.

Landau, Elaine.
Cowboys.
New York: F. Watts, 1990.

McCall, Edith.
Biography of a River: The Living Mississippi.
New York: 1990.

McFeely, William.
Frederick Douglass.
New York: Norton, 1991.

O'Neill, Richard.
Presidents of the United States.
New York: Smithmark Publishers, 1992.

Phillips, Betty Lou.
Texas.
New York: F. Watts, 1987.

Roe, Joann.
The Columbia River: An Historical Travel Guide.
Golden, Colo.: Fulcrum Publishers, 1992.

Sweeney, Edwin.
Cochise: Apache Chief.
Norman: University of Oklahoma Press, 1991.

Taylor, Marian.
Harriet Tubman.
New York: Chelsea House, 1991.

Tomchek, Ann Heinrichs.
The Hopi.
Chicago: Children's Press, 1987.

Weatherford, J. McIver.
Indian Givers: How the Indians of the Americas Transformed the World.
New York: Crown Publishers, 1988.

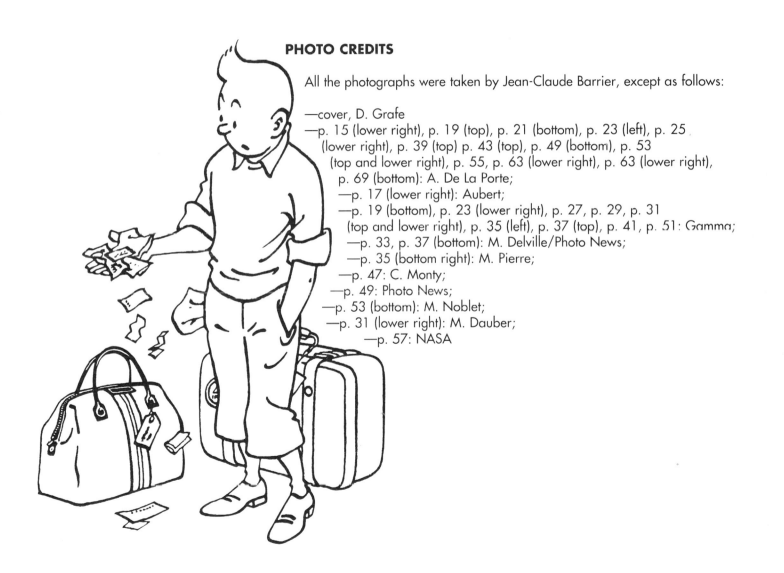

PHOTO CREDITS

All the photographs were taken by Jean-Claude Barrier, except as follows:

—cover, D. Grafe
—p. 15 (lower right), p. 19 (top), p. 21 (bottom), p. 23 (left), p. 25
  (lower right), p. 39 (top) p. 43 (top), p. 49 (bottom), p. 53
  (top and lower right), p. 55, p. 63 (lower right), p. 63 (lower right),
  p. 69 (bottom): A. De La Porte;
—p. 17 (lower right): Aubert;
—p. 19 (bottom), p. 23 (lower right), p. 27, p. 29, p. 31
  (top and lower right), p. 35 (left), p. 37 (top), p. 41, p. 51: Gamma;
—p. 33, p. 37 (bottom): M. Delville/Photo News;
—p. 35 (bottom right): M. Pierre;
—p. 47: C. Monty;
—p. 49: Photo News;
—p. 53 (bottom): M. Noblet;
—p. 31 (lower right): M. Dauber;
—p. 57: NASA

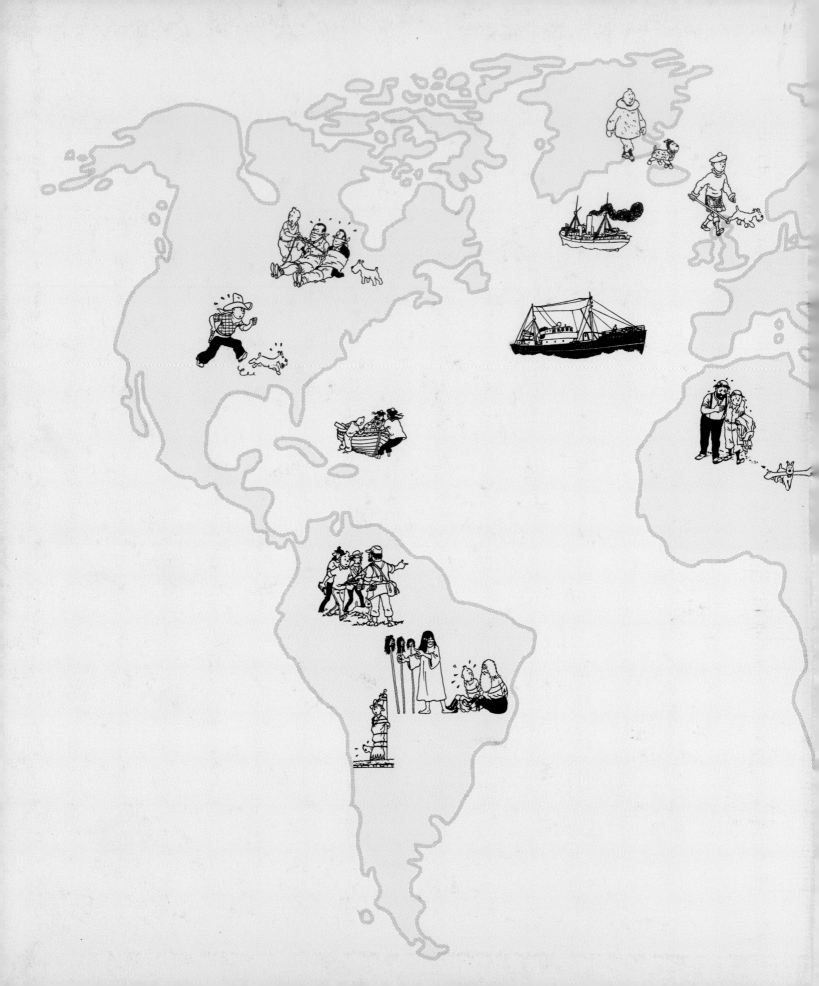